Here Comes Everybody

Here Comes Everybody

New & Selected Poems

by
Madeline Gleason

DRAWINGS BY PAUL BLAKE

Panjandrum Press 1975
San Francisco

Library of Congress Cataloging in Publication Data.

Gleason, Madeline.
    Here comes everybody.

    1. Title.
PS3513. L642H4   811'.5'2   75-37508
ISBN 0-915572-16-8 soft

Other books by Madeline Gleason:

Poems, Grabhorn/Hoyem Press, 1944.
The Metaphysical Needle, Centaur Press, 1949.
Concerto for Bell and Telephone, Unicorn Press, 1966.
Selected Poems, Dragon's Teeth Press, 1972.

Plays by Madeline Gleason:

"Why in the World", produced at the Playhouse, San Francisco,
    1960.
"Here Comes Everybody", produced at the Atheneum Fall Festival,
    1967, Mt. Tamalpais.

"Family" and "Once And Upon" first appeared in *Botteghe Oscure*
    XIX (1957).

Back cover photo by Sydney R. Goldstein, San Francisco.

This book is published by Panjandrum Press, Inc.,
a non-profit corporation. It has been funded in part by
a grant from the National Endowment for the Arts, Literature Program.

Contents

Preface by Jean Pumphrey
Dedication

Wish Springsummer
I Forgot Your Name
The Two Kingdoms
Family
The Maze
Why?
Goodbye To Home
Up And Away To Something
Ars Poetica
Let Them Not Leave
Keys
Song
The Future
The Starface
Time
Love The Phantom
Conflict
Binding Wire
Death
Once And Upon

Here Comes Everybody
  (A play for three voices)

Preface

Madeline Gleason's poetry reflects the eternal evanescence of things as they appear and disappear within the human psyche. Hers is a voice which speaks to an awareness which is deeply, unconsciously within every person.

> *"she crossed the bridge Now*
> *over the river Gone*
> *toward the place called New*
> *to begin her Once Upon. . . .*
>
> *And no trees bent down*
> *to whisper their wisdom*
> *for her becoming.*
> *Ah! New! Ah! Gone! Ah! Now!*
> *Ah! Once Upon!"*

These lines reflect the very process of consciousness, the coming and going, the life and death, the space-time transcending capacity of the human psyche. Here is poetry which speaks to the ear and to the eye within the ear.

Madeline Gleason understands the contradictions, the polarities of the human soul. Catching deeply the surface of things, she sees and she sees beyond. Her remarkable specifics reverberate. She moves and she moves us through uniquely peopled places into a God-lit world.

Jean Pumphrey
August 1975

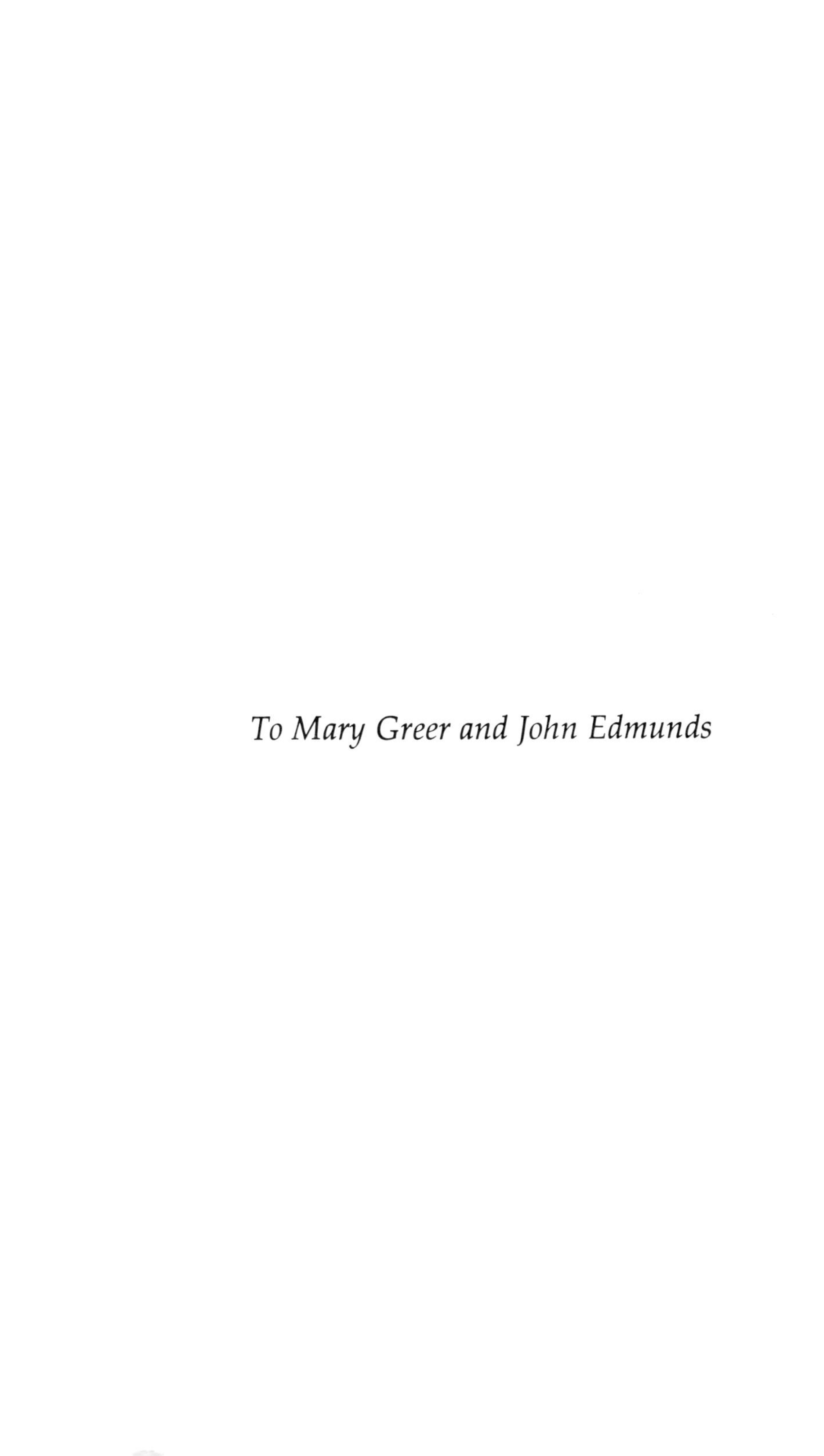

To Mary Greer and John Edmunds

Wish Springsummer

What is a wish, Father,
May I ride one?
A small wish for the small.
But when you are thought big
if not a prig,
you may ride wish SPRINGSUMMER
straight through winters
severe enough to make snowmen
of all non-wishers.
Do you know now, what a wish is dear?
No.   Yes, Father.   I do.   Don't.

Wish up, wish up, son,
Return is made at at no turning.
Forward on dreams ride dayward
until day is yours no longer,
and wish SPRINGSUMMER
gallops across morning
in the same way,
flying with the old saddle
but a new rider.

I Forgot Your Name

I waited for you
to walk with me
towards heaven.
A long way,
longer ago
than being born.

Three tones
repeated themselves:
NEAR   FAR   NEVER
struck together
they sounded an agony.

Storms began in the mind
spread to the flesh
hurricaning with wrath.

I waited for you
bore with my unblessing.
I wanted to go at once,
start on the morning
of beginning,
but I had lost all sense
of direction.

My hair grizzled,
my joints stiffened,
my legs lamed.
Which way to heaven?
And where was love,
NEAR   FAR   NEVER
I forgot your name.

The Two Kingdoms

From kingdom of loss
    to kingdom of possession
    he came, crowned to reign,
    rode in the courtly procession
    but was beaten down,
    his kingdom taken
    with his crown.

It is done again. It is done:
    in a wild tussle
    between two halves
    of his nature
    involuntary as
    a twitching muscle.

Loss is his and brings,
    plain as a boiling kettle
    sings
    time for tea,
    him to sit
    without company.

A king without kingdom
    walks by the sea,
    finds at affliction's edge
    his caves of doubt,
    washes his wounds
    in salt water
    until anguish
    is sucked out.

As he settles himself,
    the inward glance
    of his divining
    looks toward
    the new kingdom
    of possession
    to be his once more.
    He sees it clear
    as the sun shining.

It is done again. It is done:
    to pass back and forth
    between two dominions,
    either as king
    or as deposed one.

Family

What do you live by, mother?
Waiting, waiting
for my dandy-dodgers,
girls and boys,
to hang hats on bed posts
sleep one   night out of seven with me
in our high-buttoned flat
where mechanical toys
do all the work, make all the noise;
phone   to wake me from night's short death
for snip-snap, or worse, gossip;
waiting, waiting,
for jangle bell to call
from far underneath
those drowning waters of tears I weep.

What do you live by, father,
so long in the hours?
By starched shirt
by stiff competition;
by laughs and lunch with nervous men,
tight as guy wires,
but their laughter brings none close—
money alone is friend,   true friend.

What do you live by, brother?
by rule of hunting
for myself, core of me,
ego that strikes its tiresome gong
without interruption,
for the world to applaud,
pay it attention;

by hunting
for what I must find:
someone to call my face
and bid it welcome,
burn my kingdom of self,
build me kingdom of two.

What do you live by, sister?
By indecision,
blushes,   mirrors, curls,
subtraction and long division;
boys and their fearful thunder;
feeling, and swirls
of my skirt; swelling breasts;
by indecision, imitation pearls,
subtraction and long division.

What do you live by, uncle,
old soldier and drunkard?
Holy water of drink,
blessing conferred by scotch,
warmth in belly and head;
the past crated and shipped
to all the places I've been;
by winking and blinking at life,
and staring at death
who can stop my breath
at his choosing.
I sink, I shrink, I waste away.
By the holy waters of drink
I lay me down to die.

What do you live by, grandmother?
Telling, retelling,
as I knit or crochet,

sew buttons on a blouse,
how alone steps are
on pavements of day;
how alone thoughts are
on carpets at night;
single as a mouse
caught in the trap
for his cheesebite.
Telling, retelling,
how cowardice failed
to hear the song sung unafraid,
and how wounds that would speak
can only groan
to tell how alone is all alone.

The Maze

Ring clear
        Ding Dong
for Mary, Charles,
Joan and Kit,
to come through the maze
with cunning wit.

Ring loud
        Ding Dong
round and round
bramble bush,
round and round
box and yew,
already married to their fate
some sleep in the poppy bed
and never seek the exit gate.

Ring sweet
        Ding Dong
for Mary, Charles,
Joan and Kit.
Some wander lost
                lifelong
but hazards
batter into shape
those destined
to escape.

Why?

It happens

       once

and enough

       once

is too much

       once

for all time

enough is just

       Once

No More

       Good.

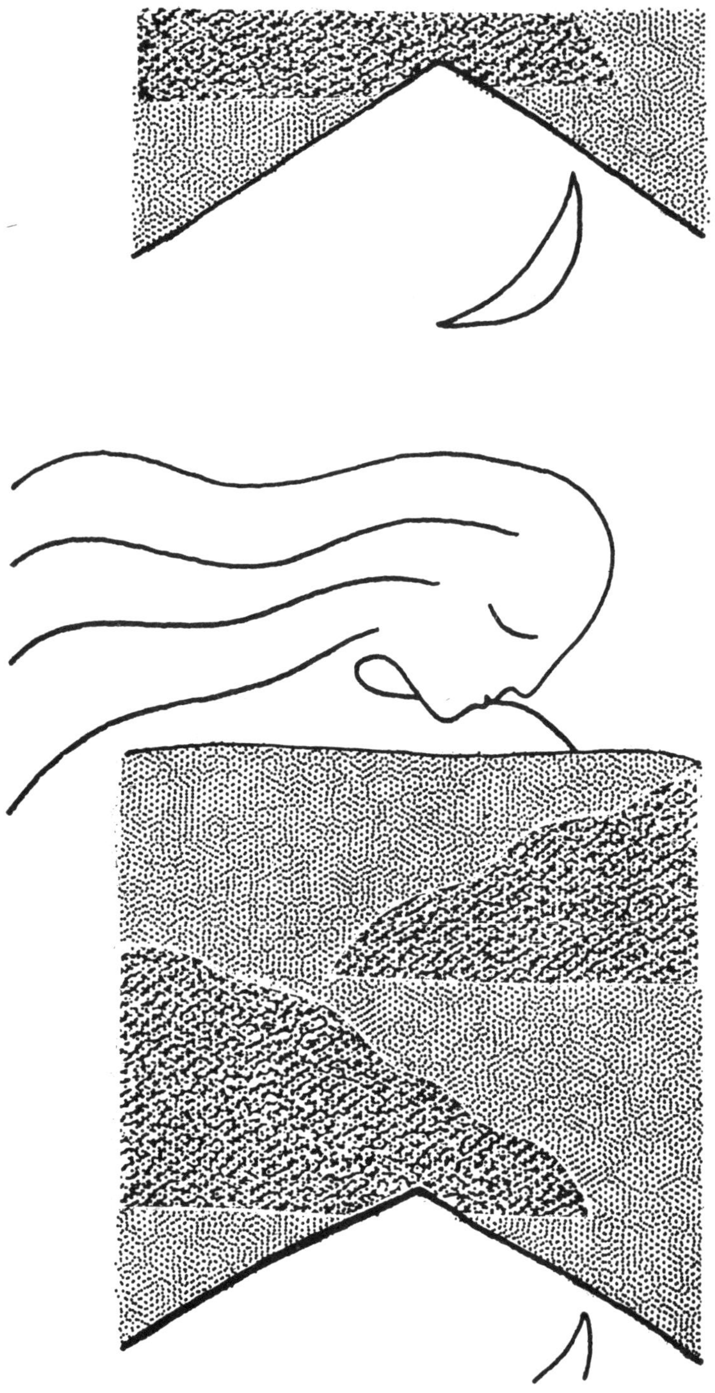

Goodbye To Home

Wave, wave, goodbye.
    Farewell, farewell
    to giggling spells,
    sudden spats,
    uninvited, hated guests,
    Uncle Ed's curses,
    Aunt Ellen's snores, and
    Mrs. Murphy, dirty old hen,
    borrowing breakfast eggs again.

Goodbye to home:
kitchen pans, walnut commode,
smack of kisses, pour of tears;
incessant clish-clash battered
ears and walls.
        Time's metronomic stroke
        beat rich in spending,
            stopped
          dead broke.

Goodbye. Goodbye.
Farewell. Farewell.
The house fell down while
mother made tea.
      Children strayed
from wading brook to open sea.
Wave, wave, farewell.
Lover from lover
           gone away
so long,   so long enough ago.
Goodbye to the children who did not
know: home is love's best dreaming bed.

Up And Away To Something

Our true home we are told resides in heaven
Where heaven is, if such a place exists,
Must be by any indirect direction,
Umpha degrees of latitudinal anxiety,
And umpha degrees of longitudinal uncertainty.
This golden chamber rich in celestial treasure,
That awaits us, rides above unseen, say:
Midmost over the Atlantic or Pacific or wherever.
So that, if we are unsure, scared, frentic,
About life, career, love, weight, age, etc.
We have been told, loosen your braces,
And tell it to heaven.

From that floating chamber,
From which has never been heard so much as a whisper,
Count on no help for your game leg, headache, ulcer,
Or any compassion for heartache or homesickness.
Tell it to heaven, you might as well
Tell it to Kelly or Goldstein.
They don't listen either, or if they do,
They don't ever, ever, ever, even drop us a line.

Ars Poetica

On Witch's night the broom hag rode,
suspending herself above the eucalyptus
she methodically inhaled the medicinal odor
then screamed other hags to the tree.

Monkeys with wrenches
shall destroy benches
on which Victorians sit.
I made this prophesy
my years ago.

                                         HAGS:

    knock, knock, knock
    antimacassars must go
    late Victorians
    fell from their benches
    on to their bottoms.
    Monkeys with wrenches
    knew what to do.

This is a solemn moment friends of Hag,
the poet tribe are all the sons of witch.
On this night preceding bloomy day
we rejoice
that every poet when he comes
is born to make a certain kind of noise.
I made this prophesy
my years ago.
    Knock knock knock knock

                                           HAGS:

With hammers and nails
and the help of their tails
monkeys built new benches

for the right sitters,
and they came
one name,
and another name.
This I foretold
exactly as it came to be.
   EXACTLY AS IT CAME TO BE
   E.P. and T.E.
   came to the bench
   looked at the tree
   took off their clothes
   and started again
   right nakedly.

The noise they made
had never before been heard
but by Angels of Poetry
and one demoniac bird.

Now there was Marianne,
with a great bag full.
I call her the syllabic queen.
Her syllables are not the *Winters'* sort
but the kind that go to court,
make a grand entrance, speak with *joie de vivre*
and after their announciation, leave
awestruck courtiers full of loving at
grace of features, figure, and coiffure,
gown, looks, lights, smiles, all perfect as her versing.

Then W.C. and W. S.
came to the tree
to undress and dress.
And Auden, master of every style
shook the airman by his alphabet,

until the age
rained down old english rhythms on·the page.
Auden, Auden,
Wystan, Hugh,   HAGS:
how many poets prayed to you.
and thought they heard an answer.

This is my prophecy
made without hitch
by me my own witch of witch.

Roar, roar full times twelve
round the zodiac Yeats will spin   HAGS:
having seen Madame Blavatsky's chain
quiver from spirits deep within.
The original two were joined by others
until the bench stretched like our space
to accommodate newcomers
And the noise they made woke the poet race.

e.e. came to the tree
e.e. lyric clown
turned the vocables upside down.

   a comic, a sport,
   a handy sort
   with his typographical bang bang
   whizz
   said this gin fizz
   of a universe   makes you
frothy as spring that isn't, that is.

This is a boisterous moment friends of Hag
they are all my boys and girls
I don't care a damn about their bald pates or curls

but the kind of noise stuffed in their owl bags
   this is the truth,
   all the truth,
   antimacassars
                              HAGS:
   had no more youth
   blow down the old poets,
   blow blow,
   every cliche must get up and go.

This is a solemn moment friends of Hag,
the last arrivals, each with owl bag,
move to the bench,
look at the tree,
remove their clothes,
and start again
full nakedly.

This is Broughton, the Playground boy.
To please the pleased.
If his songs annoy
the ear is tin,
Try once more.
Begin again, begin.
   The boy has perfect pitch.
   Anxiety is a different sound than itch.
   He'll switch you to new tunes
   on your bassoons.

This is Duncan,
with a long line delivery.
who can sing a boy into a man
and an old woman into a young.
He has a tongue
for vocables,

for starts and stops,
for the great pause
And after which drops
the word of angelic grace
HAGS:

    Here comes Duncan,
    E.P.'s sons
    his long lines tell
    of old learning
    the shadow over Eden
    and the new hell burning.

One more inhalation from the tree of health
and we will leave these poets to their wealth

I see through my lookahead
the future tree
under which shall gather new amazers
but years away my years away it is.
I leave them Broughton and Duncan.
Come hags fly,
great poets cannot lie,
this crop rid us of the curleycue
HAGS:

O duple duple and triple
good noise is good
and this good noise is new.

Let Them Not Leave

Those that have a place
Where the wild pigeon rings
With soft hammered note,
Let them not leave it.

Where the yellowhammer sings
And the wind rumbles from a basso's throat,
Let them drive a nail
In the wall
To hang up an old coat.

Where rain leaks
To a rusty pail
On the floor
And a jay creaks
On worn boards of the roof.

Those that have a place
Let them wash their hands
In the cold spring water
And never leave again.

Keys

Key at the door
And many keys to keep
In an old drawer.
Not to be used
As they once used to be.
Key keeper quiet
Till the door's ajar,
Someone on the doorstep
Throws a kiss away.
Only love's key unlocks,
Turns right.
Throw out all the rest.
Then tell the locksmith
Who it is knows best.

Song

Sing to me.
In dreams
I hear you speak.

Your face is
drawn on the walls.

In dreams
I look in your eyes,

And watch while you
Move into love with me.

Swirls of red stain
My sleeve,

Where you write
Your name,
As if,
It were fate.

Sing to me.
O sing to me.

The Future

Time, old hag,
Toothless wonder
Tell what you will
Jibe, if you must
Witch of the mechanism,
Rock-bound to tick-tock,
Hagdry till doomsday,
Tell us who sit sainted
Before sea's blue burning,
Who have tasted mouth's wine,
Read heart's book
And taken by violence
The kingdom of love's eternity.

Time, old hag,
Will you try our strength
Until muscles shrink,
Stuff us until delicate waists
Billow to shapeless sacks?
Will you carry our treasure, love,
In your withered arms
Beyond reach.

The Starface

Saved. Yet not saved.
You, like a star seen once
Float off to your distance,
Mornings and nights of distance
Riding between us a fog bank
Thru which nothing is seen
Ever, ever. Stargone,
Star to be foregone?
Nothing rising near
Hands, breast. Nothing
Shining my eyes since your face
Trailed to another sky cover,
Leaving me in the nolight of
Your going. Leaving me
With the wound of your goneness.

Time

Wrist kept ticker
Runs while I sleep.
Daily throbs with me.
Marks off my seven, twelve, five,
Midnight leap to frozen action.
Jungles, where shot fears
Rise revenant beasts,
Blurring sight of illusory clearings.

Wound, audible reminder,
You can hardly be
Forgotten or overlooked.
But once or twice,
In trance or fever,
No bell chime or tick was heard,
Only a voice telling of love
That fortune rich in tears.

Love The Phantom

Love the phantom,
Heart's ornament,
Moves in and out of
Our life's dream,
As if heaven sent.
We her dupes,
Relinquish all:
Snug, safe, nest-like ease,
To live but for her
And her wiles.
Only to find
Her love die
Or decrease.
We cannot tell
The reason why.
And we are faced with
Unwanted trials.
Adamant towards us
As stone,
She burns now
For another one.
Cold comfort this,
That the great blaze
Which shone on us
Is past, is gone.
We being no longer
Heart's desire,
Have for warmth
Only this:
Dead flame,
And remembrance,
Erstwhile fire,
Erstwhile fire.

Conflict

Down hurt and
            ache,
assaulted by racket;
pockets and belly
                empty;
swimming the filth of mind's
rotten city;   he told the door closed
on his face: Open!   Admit me!

Against the rusting hinge, he prayed
the wind;   swing back the wood;
pull me inside that room where light falls
loving on the bare floor.

Undone by himself; himself the
sacrifice; he strained to be hacked
to bits — halved; quartered — his city
                        razed.

Then he, fresh minted by touch
of some golden saint
                would arise to secure
a new, another self, in the loving light.

Binding Wire

Struggle free
from binding wire
that cables the past:
those friends
who furnished the wire
to further their ends.

Struggle free
from twisted thoughts
that twist the way;
cruise of a smile
on a mouth
at bay.

Struggle free
from Sunday blues
of old phone calls;
of love that draws away
from the fire
and will not warm,
will not warm.
Last, lost, cold companion!

Struggle free
from whatever it was
first tightened the wire,
and still can do it
and still does.

Death

Death is
    between tick and tock
    where no speech is,
    no crying sound,
no I,
no thou,
but each
    wrapped in his single fold,
asleep, undreamed, undreaming.
The impasse, gulfed with vacuity.
And we have
      nothing,
      or have
an eternity of sound,
speech inflamed
        to such new
        beginnings, as
        none ever knew, or
in his fire, records.

Death is
    not any this
      or that,
   only
      light stabbed;
fullness emptied out.

The usher sleep,
    aisles us to the
      appointed place.

We dare death
        even in the lover's bed.
        And love, starred,
        mooned, sunned to
            desire's excess
in kissing;   flies deathward
                in ecstasy.
                    Demands the test of
                        exile
            from spirit, instinct and
                        the body's house.

Once And Upon

Cross at the morning
and at waking,
with a mourning for summer,
she crossed the bridge Now
over the river Gone
toward the place called New
to begin her Once Upon.

Once and Upon
daddy long legs
walked in a web of work
for my sisters and me,
as Mother spun round
with silver knives and forks
in a shining of pans,
a wash of mondays
and plans
for our lives ten thousand weeks.

To cross the bridge Now
over the river Gone
toward the place called New
to begin her Once Upon,
in a mourning for summer, she moved
to write her right becoming
and find her true beloved.

Snippets and tags of Gone,
criss-crossed as retold,
beggared the strumming
of fresh rhythms
that should have stirred her becoming.

Once and Upon
she ate the plum
and from a full mouth
disgorged the pit
into her hand
while Mother spun as she canned
peach and plum in season —
the land, holy Mother to
the plentiful fruit.

To cross.
But where should her steps lead
away from the river?

Through a desert she hurried,
thirsting she ran
to reach becoming,
passed three water holes
but never saw them,
so eager was she to reach
outward evidence
of her inward drawing.

Sisters of grace,
comely, sea-washed,
with blond shell hair and skin,
whirling with intermittent passion
amidst daddy long legs
and Mother awash
among the underthings,
boys shouting and running,
swaggering and dying
for the sisters' charms.
AMEN!

Tops a-spin in a dying dance.
Yoo Hoo, Fatty! Buck!
Hi, Pete! Hello, old Gene!

Cross at the morning
summer crossed with the beginning
of gold,
a sea of brown leaves swirling.

And no trees bent down
to whisper their wisdom
for her becoming.
Ah! New! Ah! Gone! Ah! Now!
Ah! Once Upon!

Here Comes Everybody

FIRST VOICE: Thrones! Powers!

SECOND VOICE: Dominations!

THIRD VOICE: Dominations! In sport we enter the foreground scalping time with rocket development.

FIRST: Abide with me fast falls. . . .

SECOND: Heard a ghost say coast with me in this disarmament plan.

THIRD: Plan. Plan. Years ahead against dismemberment. Lifetime members assured a policy of. . . .

FIRST AND SECOND: Fox, Fox, Foxy fox. Giants, Dodgers, Red Sox.

THIRD: Sex throws ball, makes hit, love is game. Game all.

FIRST AND THIRD: Come let us sport and play, sport and play. Come let us sport and play!

SECOND: Dominations! Principalities!

THIRD: Unless you see signs and wonders, you do not believe.

SECOND: In whom we have our redemption. . . .

FIRST sings, keeps on singing during Second's voice speech: come let us sport and play.

SECOND VOICE, chanting: When the unclean spirit has gone out of a man he roams through waterless places in search of a resting place and finding none, he says, I will return to my house. . . When he comes he finds the place swept. He goes and takes seven other spirits more evil than himself. . . They enter in and the last state of that man becomes worse than the first.

THIRD: Am coming. Already am with you. Pack hunts. Barks. Yells. Tractors. Factory sirens. Backaches, Tapdrips. Screams.

FIRST: The sparrow hath found herself a house and the turtle a nest, where she may lay her young ones.

SECOND: Colossus of sound vibrating! Exploding! Breaking open shoulders. Deal! Deal!

THIRD: The sparrow hath found herself a house and the turtle a nest, where she may lay her young ones. . . .

SECOND: Deal, deal, contract binding.

FIRST: Concrete cracking! Deal!

THIRD: Flush for you, you lucky stiff. Chuff, chugg.

FIRST: Pint porter wash, sluice gravey. Dab wet rag on pants near pocket. Clean, clean greasy gravey.

SECOND: Grave, wet, horrible. Simmer me in summer with my buttons undone. What a handsome tan. What a handy hairy. . . . Lo! Good looking reluctant MAAAANN.

FIRST: Will you? Will you? Will you? O Bill you mustn't cheat on me no more! Bucky boy, my big eared muscled kid. Don't do it no more!

SECOND: Shaaaaatup!

FIRST: Sweetheart, I loved long and long and grew to be out of fashion like an old song.

SECOND: Why won't you? O Christ, good God. Mary pray hard. I can't believe he's that bigga crook. Took me for whore. Christ, you tell God. Mary tell'im. I can't take no more.

THIRD: Sir, come down before my child dies.

FIRST: Mary, tell'im, I can't take no more. "O love, how strangely sweet are thy weak passions. That love and joy could meet in self same fashion. O love, how strangely sweet. . . ."

SECOND & THIRD: Sir, come down before my son dies. . . .

SECOND: Baby can't tell. Baby won't tell, even when he's grown up. Can't penetrate baby's shell: tabulate his errors, miscalculations: count the fallen angels inhabit his hell.

Pause

FIRST: Sir, come down. . . .

SECOND: He's up I tell you. He got up. Threw his pillow at his young sister. He's hollerin. . . . He's up. I tell you. It's him running meet his pa come home five o'clock from shipyards.

FIRST: Warm up! Speed up!

SECOND: Warm up! Speed up! Race that engine!

FIRST: He said: go thy way, thy son liveth!

SECOND AND THIRD: My heart is ready. Alleu! Alleu! I sleep, but my heart watches.

FIRST: No. Machine. No. Machine. Yeh! IBM was at fault. We made the mistake. No machine better than the person who feeds it.

THIRD: IBM is my delight. IBM is my desire. IBM is my heart of gold. Who but my IBM?

SECOND, colloquial tone: Touch of the keys, dividends punched. Lucky ones get that little extra, that little extra, helps so much. I sleep but my heart watches.

THIRD: Ill, but mother in best miltown mode iterates bland maxims in becalmed meditation.

FIRST: Idleness breeds melancholy.

SECOND: Ill, but mother . . . inviolate behind muteness. Intense batement light modulations . . . That little extra . . . That helps so much. . . .

THIRD: I sleep, but my heart watches. Child came. Name bestowed by angel. O God whodidst. . . .

FIRST: Lo! Hi! Yah! Drive over now. You could see the baby. O he's not walking yet. Grandma said I could walk at nine months. Yah! Unhuh! Unhuh! Unhuh! Ooooooooo! Unhuh! Huh? Unhuh! Bye.

SECOND AND THIRD: What wouldst thou that I do for thee. . . ?

FIRST: That I might see . . . see . . . see . . . see. . . !

SECOND: Lookin, lookin, lookin, lookin, lookin.

THIRD: What'd I find? Nothin. Great big broad assed nothin. I should known you was worst sonbitch trot round my front back door. Don't come back no more. I'm sick sight of you.

FIRST AND SECOND: Lookin. Lookin. Lookin. Lookin. What you lookin for, honey?

THIRD: Brand new he. Shiney as bumble bee andddddd sweety for me. Buzz me baby. Buzz me.

FIRST, sings: "Lost is my quiet, forever. Forever lost is my quiet. Lost is my quiet, forever . . . Lost, lost, life's happiest part. . . ."

SECOND: Love extinguished, put out like a light in the nighttime. Imponderables; blackout; stabbing; dead carcases dragged round and round self's precipices; through valleys; over stagnant waters; crags; alleys; the beaten lie bleeding untended.

THIRD, sings: Lost, lost, life's happiest part. Forever. Forever. My quiet. . . .

FIRST: Seasonable, vulnerable. He was he, my human love. How could he be other than he was? "Forever, forever, lost is my quiet . . . ."

THIRD: Little did he know, how could he guess. He'd press the grapes of hell in hell.

SECOND: What happens when we die, do you think?

FIRST: We perish.

SECOND: That's all there is to it?

THIRD: Yeh! Yeh! Perish.

SECOND: Perish? What then?

THIRD: What you want me to say? Why, we perish into the higher after.

FIRST: "Now the seventh evening arose in Eden."

SECOND: Beautiful sounds. *Magnifique.* Sonorous.

THIRD: I like that! Perish into the higher after. What a rickety pisspot this one is. Behind and around. Never directly in.

FIRST: Behind your behind. To plant a great glutton of a kick square in the middle of. . . .

THIRD: Ha! Perish into the higher after. . . !

FIRST: He hath clothed me in garments of salvation. . . . I will greatly rejoice in the Lord. . . .

SECOND: I will greatly rejoice. He hath covered me

as a bride adorned with her jewels. . . .

THIRD: He hath clothed me . . . I·will greatly
rejoice. . . .

SECOND: Shall I find it? I shall not find it. Find it. By
light of my pickus pokus.

FIRST: You shall bekind it. By right of bogus logos.

THIRD: You shall beknight it. By right of your august
lotus.

FIRST AND THIRD: Time. Time. Prime number. True
north. Compass true north. Best born do not go forth to
beg or dig.

SECOND: Unable to table resolution until the next,
next, next, next. . . .

THIRD: I will not lean over your shoulder to read
Krishnamurti.

FIRST: Angel Gabriel was sent to a town called
Nazareth.

SECOND: Many are called. Few get up. Jokes, pokes
in the eye. Jokes. Many are cold, few are. . . .

THIRD: Frozen food packages so gaily, daily I pick
you, unfreeze creamy goodness. Heat in a small boiling,
boiling . . . over a hotsy flame. . . .

FIRST: Whose muse, often harsh, intransigent.
Delivers cruel punishing body blows. . . .

SECOND: Fires of the world. Purged. Newborn. Old
trimmings blown away in the heart's smoke. The typist
screameth not though her fires are dying. . . .

THIRD: Some cold days coming . . . Drowsy,
fatigued. Mock bloom on youth's cheek bones . . . What
a high polish . . . Once . . . moulded with strength,
grace . . . Once.

FIRST: Fires of the world. . . .

SECOND AND THIRD, nostalgic: Purged. Old
trimmings. Those hands . . . Once . . . Don't touch it.
Defiles . . . Desecrates . . . Those hands . . . Enamelled
nails . . . Once . . . Delicate phalanges. . . .

FIRST: Bring my gloves, Martha. Hurry! Not those
you fool!

THIRD: Useless gloves for amputated hands!

SECOND: I'll fire that kid. Only one thing on his mind. He ought to be out selling. Sell himself! He can do that. He's got those girls all worked up over. . . .

FIRST: Nothing lost. Nothing be starved for want of love. The web holding our clasped hands.

THIRD: Is man more interesting than God?

SECOND: "I burn with all the desires of my unconquered flesh. It is ardor of the spirit that I ought to feel: but it is the flesh, desire, laziness, idleness, and sleepiness that possess me."

FIRST: IBM is my heart of gold. Who but my IBM?

THIRD: The bookkeeper singeth not in his office cage. Bent over his slanting counter, making careful marks until his ledgers fill. . . . He hangs up his hat; his coat. Daily he swallows the boss who sticks in his throat.

FIRST: Bookkeeper singeth not in this office cage . . . Singeth not . . . singeth not. . . .

THIRD: A rough game. Swaying with the earth's unfelt motion . . . A rough game. Played hard against silk-swathed opponents. . . .

SECOND: I burn with all the ardour of . . . in sleepless nights; in fastings; in knowledge; in long-sufferings; in kindness; in the holy spirit; in unaffected love. . . .

THIRD: See that man! That man!

SECOND: Where?

FIRST: That one there!

THIRD: What wouldst thou that I should do for thee?

SECOND: This morning, that guy's walkin down Post Street. Tap tapping white cane. Pushing it round curb, getting ready to cross.

FIRST: Any old signal from you, duck. Just try me. Give me the eye. . . .

SECOND: Listen, if you come across me act like you never seen me. I gotta some very own specially, my potatoes to fry.

THIRD: Which guy?

SECOND: That little stiff sitting over there cryin. What hell he's cryin for? He seen! Never seen before.

FIRST: Yah! This morning seen his own mother. He went bugs: passed out cold. Come to with his mother standing there. She kept sayin: Tommy, my little Tommy.

THIRD: He's waitin for his uncle to take him home. Seen. Sumpin! O God! Mother. O God, he said, he seen!

SECOND: Nothing lost. Nothing be starved for want of love . . . Kindness frozen in the act of unresponsiveness. Cruelty. Retreat.

FIRST: Fall from heights of favors, and delicacies, to dregs and slops. Why did she do it? Why? Why?

THIRD: Jerry, if you leave this house . . . Please go to blazes. Don't bother to come. . . .

FIRST: I finished this off months ago. Ice-sheet, ice spar, ice cap. Glassey eyed virago, manhater, housebreaker, man-cheater. You ice quaked this place until it convulsed.

THIRD: Jerry, I'm warning you. If you leave this house. . . .

SECOND: "He said: Go call thy husband . . . The woman answered: I have no husband . . . And he said to her: Thou hast well said, I have no husband. Thou hast had five, and he whom thou now hast is not thy husband. . . ."

FIRST: In sleepless nights;   in fastings;   in knowledge;   in long sufferings;   in kindness;   in the holy spirit;   in unaffected love. . . .

THIRD: Ask Father, son, Holy Ghost, what love is that men. . . .

FIRST: Is Man more interesting than God?

SECOND: Come on! Come on!

THIRD, sings: Drink to me only with thine eyes. . . .

SECOND: Have something. Do you good. Remember Archie. He went crazy when Janet trecked off with that Ames Jo. What do we let ourselves in for? Home makers.

Baby getters. Home makers . . . Home.

FIRST, sings: Hills of home. O hills of home. . . .

SECOND: Hells of home . . . Archie came one night last September . . . Drunk. A sight . . . Drink up . . . Good for sole survivor of marriage ship. Went down in a quarreling sea. No help at hand. Yelled their heads off. But she couldn't buck that storm. . . .

FIRST: Come on, drink. Warm up inside.

THIRD, sings: Keep the home boys burning. . . .

SECOND: She was your bride, now she's somebody else's bride. Why'd we take it so hard? Drink, drink to me only . . . Leave a kiss within the cup.

FIRST: Bottoms up. Bottoms up, boys. Bottoms up! *(sings)* Keep the home boys burning. . . .

THIRD: He said unto her: If thou knewest the gift of God and who it is that saith 'Give me to drink': thou wouldst have asked of him . . . living water . . . a well of water springing up into everlasting life.

THIRD: Thrones! Dominations! Powers!

SECOND: In anguish, anguish, we enter the background. Pushing time. Slicing it juicy for this and that. Mourning the morning. *(sings).* Time on my hands . . . That lusty jolly Chaucerian spring . . . All lovers in the spring. . . .

FIRST With a hey and a ho and hey nonny. Pretty ringtime. Springtime. All lovers in the spring. Springtime. . . .

THIRD: Pretty ringtime springtime. Ho. Nonny. Hey. Jolly joyous, lusty Chaucerian springtime. O hey nonny no.

SECOND: Springtime. No. No. No. No. Not. Enter the background. . . .

THIRD: Where does it go? It flows away with the waters, that promised to stand like rock. . . .

FIRST: In anguish, anguish we enter the background . . . Floweth away. . . .

SECOND: In these lay a great multitude of impotent folk, blind, halt, withered, waiting for the moving of. . . .

FIRST: For an angel went down at a certain season into

the pool and troubled the water. . . .

THIRD: Principalities! Dominations!

FIRST: Light up time! Light up a Plucky. Light.
Light. . . .

SECOND: Day dreamed me downside, upside, right side
up, backside. Hole in one. Tore the air. Clawed it. Found
him like that, poor thing! Close to it. Another few minutes.

THIRD: Light up time. Light up a Plucky . . . Light up
time. . .

FIRST: I am the way, the truth and the. . . .

THIRD: Go back the same way you came. Can you find
the way back?

SECOND: "We may not lightly abandon the castle, the
planet and the crimson cloud, and hope to retain the eye,
its retina, and the brain."

THIRD: Way you came. Why did you . . . Go back.
Come back . . . Go back. Come back. . . .

THIRD: Well, if you're young, you can take it. It's youth
all the way. What do you need anything more'en enough.

FIRST: Listen you little tramp. That's what Dad calls you.

THIRD, sings: Tramp, tramp, tramp the boys are
marching. . . .

FIRST: Marching up to your room at night, taking the
backstairs way. You think Dad and I was born minute ago?
You quit this or get away from this house.

THIRD, sings: Get away little trampie, get away. . . .

SECOND: It's a lie, Ma. Honest God, I always tell you
t'truth. It was only once. Johnny, he needed help with his
algebra. Honest God, Ma. God's truth. You tell Dad. I'm
not bad, Ma. . . .

FIRST, sings: "At that bedside kneeleth a may, and she
weepeth both night and day. In that room there standeth a
stone. Corpus Christe written thereon. . . .

THIRD: These things I command you: that you love one
another.

SECOND: Over the hill the moon in meditation. On her
moving ambit. Beneath her lovers fill their mouths with

kisses: twang like plucked strings with high jangle.

FIRST: These things I command you: that you love one another.

THIRD: It can't last long. It won't last long. They please each other a little while. Things go wrong. Light goes out: bell clapper breaks: fiddle strings snap. . . .

FIRST: Little joy fountain . . . tinkling drops . . . dry up.

SECOND AND THIRD: Little joy fountain . . . tinkling drops . . . Dries up. Drip. Drop. Drop. Drop. Drop.

FIRST: Stop. I don't feel like kissing you. That's what! I don't feel like . . . Stop!

SECOND: Won't you ever grow up?

THIRD: He said: Whoever shall receive this child in my name receiveth me. . . .

FIRST: Children spin their blond headtops in skip - run - sheep - hide - seek - blind man's bluff.

THIRD: This child in my name . . . A great big blubbery baby.

SECOND: Love you? All that stuff! Who swore he wouldn't get bored? With you, darling, it'll last, go on and on. My bon bon, sweet, dearest sweet. Under the sheets . . . Forever . . . My hon. . . .

THIRD: Who was that ladle I seen you eating with the other night? That wasn't no ladle. That was my knife.

FIRST: Jokes, pokes in the eye, jokes. What did the telegram say, Bert?

THIRD: O my wife's mother died. She wanta know should she embalm, bury or cremate. I told her, God's sake, embalm, bury and cremate. Take no chances. . . .

FIRST: Jokes. Jokes. My funny bone's sore. You tickle my under. . . .

SECOND: Many are called but . . . Change. Change of pace. Give my old days to the garbage man. Don't I pay him enough. Go on dump 'em in the trash can.

FIRST: Where them damned kids? I told em: Be in by six. You sit there airing your big feet. Get outta street. Get them kids in here, big lummox. I'd like burn you off my

skin like that doc rid me my warts. Gwan, get them kids in
here. . . .

SECOND: These things I command you.

THIRD: Take nothing for your journey . . . Light up
time.

FIRST: Can't you see where you're going, Mack?

THIRD: Light up. "Ether is identified with the ether
whose wave disturbances constitute light: furthermore . . .
there are reasons . . . Light . . . Electromagnetic
disturbances governed by. . . ."

SECOND: Take nothing for your journey. *(sings)* "O
gentle folk you may behold and see how I lie here,
sometime a mighty knight. The end of joy and all
prosperity is death at last. Thorough his course and
length. . . ."

THIRD: Holy!   Holy!   Holy!   Lord God of Hosts!

FIRST: Children with their daisy chains . . . Break the
chains bind them to childhood.

THIRD: I am the way . . . It's a long way, skip with the
fairies. Bow to the Queen. O Mother, he's the nicest boy in
class.

SECOND: Now look here, Miss. Settle down with those
books. If that report card isn't. . . .

FIRST: Mother. . . !

THIRD: Do what I say. Life is a book, so learn to read it.
Not just a peek, better take a good look.

FIRST When I was your age. . . .

SECOND: Page after page . . . mountains of print . . . .
learn . . . learn . . . you'll fry, burn . . . sizzle . . . burn . . .
erase my memories.

FIRST: Bless my disdain.

THIRD: My rose of flowers. My youth, farewell!

SECOND: Thrones! Dominations! Principalities!

THIRD, sings: "After the day, there cometh the long
night. And though the day be never so bright, at last the
bell ringeth to eventide."

FIRST: A long way off. Challenge. Support me. A long

way off. Make those hours count for something. Count.
Count.

THIRD: I'm up to seventy-five now. How long will I live,
Mother?

SECOND: Why, nobody knows but the good Lord.

FIRST: Mother?

THIRD: A long long time, dear. Please God.

FIRST AND SECOND: Count, count, count, count, count,
count, count, count. . . .

THIRD: You'll make something of yourself. That's one
thing I know for certain.

FIRST: How do you know?

SECOND: I just do, that's all.

SECOND AND THRID: Count, count, count, count,
count, count, count, count, count, count, count, count. . . .

FIRST: Through children's game, through night way. Up
. . . into . . . away from . . . on top of . . . back to . . .
children's game . . . night way. Thunder cry me!

SECOND: Sweetheart ever leaving! That sun is!

THIRD: In the beginning . . . in water under death. . . .

SECOND: Word's brush . . . paint speaks. . . .

FIRST: Sound's fly lark . . . sing head. Night of all
thine is. . . .

THIRD: And the music . . . Omen . . . O man. . . .

SECOND: Masters be there . . . Wait all, always . . . with
grieving joy. . . .

FIRST, SECOND, THIRD: The terrible vine is art. Leap,
sing, shout. Face face. Be first. Choose. One is . . . Begin.
Bravo. Hey! Hi! Ho! Dante . . . Hey! Hi! Ho! Columbus . . .
Hey! Hi! Ho! Fulton.

FIRST: One is.

SECOND: Flight to alone. Shaking lights dance.

THIRD: Hey! Hi! Ho! One.

FIRST, SECOND, THIRD: Bravo! Holy! Holy! Holy! Lord
God of Hosts!